DATE			

Table of Contents

Library of Congress Cataloging-in-Publication Data
Gonzalez, Christina.
  [Pueblo Inca. English]
  Inca civilization / by Christina Gonzalez.
    p. cm. — (The World heritage)
  Includes index.
  Summary: Highlights the cultural achievements, both material and spiritual, of
the ancient Incas.
  ISBN 0-516-08380-5
  1. Incas—Juvenile literature. [1. Incas. 2. Indians of South America.] I. Title.
II. Series.
F3429.G6813 1993
984'.01—dc20
                                                         92-37021
                                                             CIP
                                                             AC

El Pueblo Inca: © INCAFO S.A./Ediciones S.M./UNESCO 1990
Inca Civilization: © Childrens Press, Inc./UNESCO 1993

ISBN (UNESCO) 92-3-102684-1
ISBN (Childrens Press) 0-516-08380-5

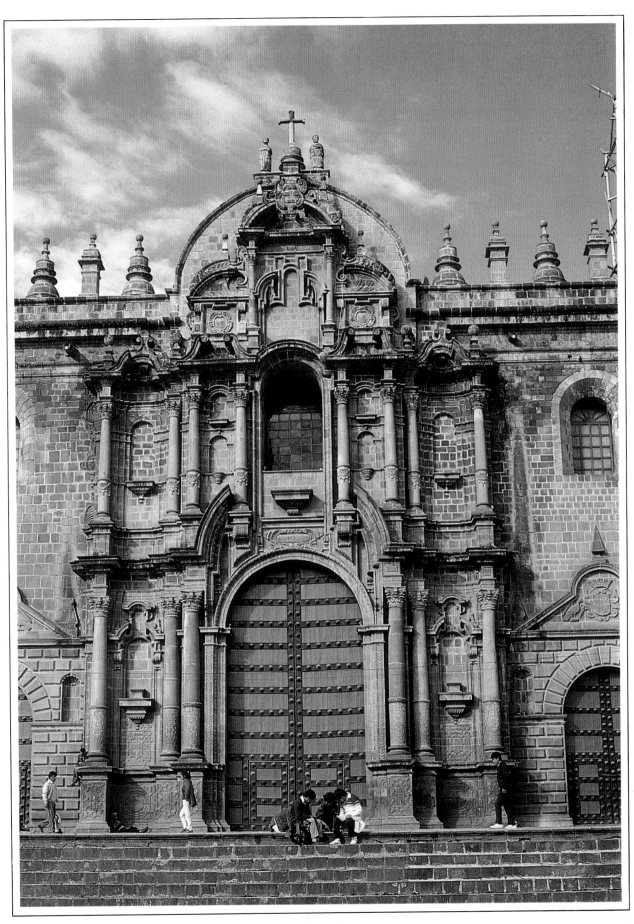

Inca Civilization

In 1532, Francisco Pizarro captured the Inca emperor Atahualpa. With that event began the collapse of the Inca Empire. This was the last of the great civilizations that had flourished in the Americas before the arrival of Christopher Columbus.

At the time of the Spanish conquest, the Inca Empire extended throughout the Andes Mountain region of what is now South America. In their Quechua language, the Inca called their empire the Tahuantinsuyu— "the Kingdom of the Four Regions of the Universe."

From north to south, the Inca Empire reached from present-day Colombia, through Ecuador, Peru, and Bolivia, down to Chile and Argentina. It stretched west from the Amazon Basin to the Pacific Ocean. The empire was ruled by the Sapa Inca, the "Son of the Sun." From Cuzco, the capital of the empire, he wielded absolute power over his enormous kingdom.

The Inca Empire was the end of a long process of cultural change. Over hundreds of years, distinct culture groups settled in the Andean region. They struggled to adapt to the difficulties of life in the mountains. Of all these groups, the Incas finally ruled supreme. They built a powerful state that made important cultural achievements, both material and spiritual.

Capital of the Empire of the Sun

Cuzco was the capital of the Inca Empire. Though it was conquered by the Spaniards in 1533, the city still preserves many traces of the Pre-Columbian era. Many of its ancient walls were used to support later colonial buildings. This is the pattern that can be seen in the photo, which shows a wall of the famous Coricancha, or Temple of the Sun. Within this temple, the people worshiped a great sun-like disk of gold and precious stones.

The Inca Nation and Its History

To learn about Inca history, we cannot turn to documents written by the Incas themselves. They had no system of writing. Instead, they passed on their traditions through stories handed down from generation to generation.

Most of what we know about the Incas comes from the accounts of sixteenth-century Spanish *conquistadores*, or conquerors. The *conquistadores* wrote down everything they observed about the customs, daily life, social structure, and economy of the Inca Empire. They also wrote down many of its traditional stories and legends.

The origin of the Inca nation is shrouded in legend. One story tells of a great dynasty that reigned until the fall of the empire. Its founders were a married brother and sister, Manco Cápac and Mama Ocllo. They came to the valley of Cuzco (today a Peruvian city) from somewhere near Lake Titicaca, a mountain lake at the border of Peru and Bolivia. Their arrival marks the beginning of civilized life for the Incas. Before this was an obscure era of disorder and warfare.

This myth might help to explain how a small ethnic group settled in the region where the Inca capital would one day stand. Gradually, this group extended its power over neighboring peoples, until they were united under one vast empire. This they named the Tahuantinsuyu.

According to Inca tradition, twelve monarchs reigned from the beginning of the empire until the Spanish conquest. But the true history of Tahuantinsuyu dates only from the eighth sovereign—the Inca Viracocha—who reigned early in the fifteenth century. Actual Inca history covers barely one hundred years. But in this brief time rose one of the world's greatest civilizations.

Before the reign of Viracocha, we know only that the Incas were involved in a series of conflicts with neighboring tribes. In these wars, the Incas came to dominate their neighbors. However, they did not rely upon force alone to strengthen their empire.

They also offered gifts to the chiefs of neighboring tribes. Through arranged marriages, they were able to make alliances with other groups. Only when diplomacy failed did soldiers appear on the scene.

The Inca Pachacuti, Viracocha's son, extended his domain from the Andean plateau to the Pacific coast. To the newly conquered lands, he brought a system of law and order that would be the basis of the empire's development.

The Incas, Master Stone Masons

Many of the people who live in Cuzco today (*top photo*) are direct descendants of the Incas. The Inca domain once reached throughout the Andean region from Colombia to Chile and from the Amazon Basin to the Pacific. Inca architecture was based on a method of stacking blocks of granite one upon another, with no mortar to hold them together. In the lower photo is a portion of one of the walls that still stand in modern Cuzco. The stone in the center is known as "The Stone of the Twelve Angles." The anonymous workman was, without doubt, a master stone mason.

The Lost City

The fortress of Machu Picchu, located about 8,530 feet (2,600 meters) above sea level, was discovered by the archaeologist Hiram Bingham in 1911. This photograph shows a panoramic view of the site, with the peak of Huayna Picchu in the background. The "Lost City of the Incas," like the adventurous Bingham himself, is surrounded by mysteries that remain unsolved today. Who built Machu Picchu? When was the construction completed? Who lived there? The city's very name is unknown, for the name Machu Picchu has only recently come into use. The answers to these questions are buried in myths as dense as the vegetation that has overgrown the ruins.

The Inca Pachacuti was followed by Tupac Inca Yupanqui. This sovereign expanded the borders of Tahuantinsuyu to embrace present-day Colombia and Chile. Next came the rule of Huayna Cápac. At his death in 1530, the kingdom was divided between his sons Atahualpa and Huaskar.

Unfortunately, the two brothers fell into a bloody war over which of them should rule supreme. The Spaniards, led by Francisco Pizarro, took advantage of the hatred and fighting to carry out their plan for the conquest of the Incas.

Nevertheless, the Spanish conquest was neither easy nor rapid. Inca resistance was stubborn, though disorganized because of the civil war. After Atahualpa was captured and condemned to death, the empire began to topple. Pizarro recognized Manco II, another of the sons of Huayna Cápac, as the legitimate sovereign. Unhappy with the actions of the *conquistadores*, Manco II held Cuzco under siege.

Views of the Abyss

Because of Machu Picchu's strategic location, it remained hidden until the beginning of the twentieth century. As seen in the top photo, the city stands in a wild landscape of steep mountains and yawning canyons, crisscrossed by the Rio Urubamba. The lower photo shows a vicuna. Llamas, alpacas, guanacos, and vicunas are the main domestic animals in this region. The Incas used their wool and meat. They even used the animals' droppings as fertilizer and fuel. The llama provided so many resources that the Incas treated it as a sacred being, a gift from the gods.

Timeline of Inca History

Before the 12th Century. Founding of the Inca dynasty by Manco Cápac. Legendary period.

End of the 12th Century to Beginning of the 13th Century. Kingdom of Roca Yupanqui. Neighboring peoples are subdued.

13th Century. Reign of Mayta Cápac. The Incas expand to the west and south.

Beginning of the 14th Century. Reign of Inca-Roca. War with the Chancas Indians.

14th Century. Kingdom of Yahuar-Huacoc, who was forced to abdicate after defeat by the Chancas.

Beginning of the 15th Century. Kingdom of the Inca Viracocha. The war with the Chancas continues. The Inca Empire expands farther to the north and south.

1438–1471 (?). Reign of Inca Pachacutec, who finally defeats the Chancas. Inca sovereignty is recognized from the Andean plateau to the Pacific coast.

After 1471. Reign of Tupac Yupanqui. The empire is at its height.

Beginning of the 16th Century. Kingdom of the last grand Inca, Huayna Cápac.

1530. Death of Huayna Cápac. The empire is divided between his sons Atahualpa and Huaskar. Civil war begins.

1532. Capture and death of Atahualpa by the Spaniards, led by Francisco Pizarro. The empire begins to disintegrate.

1535. The Spaniards are held under siege in the city of Cuzco.

1572. The last Inca, Tupac Amaru, is captured by the Spaniards.

End of the Inca Empire.

The most elite members of Inca society were the nobles, or *orejones*. In Spanish, *orejón* means "big-eared." The orejones were named for their enormous earlobes, which were stretched out of shape by the heavy ornaments they wore as earrings.

Another privileged social group were the *acllas*, or chosen women. From the time they were very young, they received a painstaking education, which included education into secret religious rituals.

Some *acllas* married members of the nobility or the sovereign himself. Others devoted their lives to the care of the temples, living in adjoining buildings. They were known as *mamacones*, or Virgins of the Sun.

The religious classes of people and the social classes were completely separate, although both were headed by the sovereign. The large priestly class was led by one high priest. He lived a life of constant meditation, never ate meat, and drank only water. On ceremonial occasions, he wore a special tiara decorated with feathers and a sun of gold. His suit was made of fine white wool with red embroidery, and it sparkled with precious stones and gold ornaments.

Another class was that of the *mitimaes*, or transplants. When a new territory was added to the empire, groups of people were "transplanted" there to help spread the Incas' customs and cultural traditions. This practice also helped to guarantee the security of the empire.

At the bottom of the social scale were the *hatunruna*, the common people who worked the land. The masses were the great motor of the state. Through their labor, they maintained the unproductive elite.

The Four Regions of the Universe

The Inca Empire was known as Tahuantinsuyu, which in the Quechua language means "The Kingdom of the Four Regions of the Universe." These regions were the Chinchasuyu (to the north), the Collasuyu (to the south), the Antisuyu (to the east), and the Contisuyu (to the west). On the map, we see the extent of the Inca Empire before Pizarro's conquest.

The first building in Machu Picchu is the fortified tower shown at the lower right. Built on an enormous rock, it has two trapezoid-shaped windows and eight interior recesses.

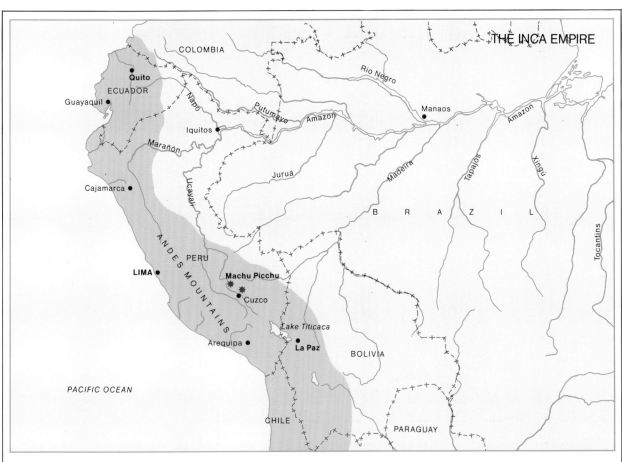

THE INCA EMPIRE

The *hatunruna* were grouped in *ayllus*, or clans. A clan consisted of the descendants of a single ancestor, real or imaginary. Each clan owned and worked a piece of land communally. They also worshiped the special gods that protected the clan and its territory. The peasant family was monogamous — each man had only one wife — and its members were not allowed to move from one residence to another. The people were strictly controlled by means of an elaborate, periodic census.

The Economy

The economy of the Inca Empire was based on a careful use of their sparse natural resources. The Incas were able to meet their basic needs and to store some surplus food for hard times.

It was difficult to grow crops in the Incas' high, dry environment. To create cropland from the steep mountainsides, they built step-like terraces. They also constructed irrigation canals. These canals were sometimes as much as 60 miles (100 kilometers) long.

The land that could be cultivated was divided into three parts: the lands of the Sun, the lands of the Inca, and the lands of the Community.

The Former Temple of the Sun

As often happens in Latin America, many churches in Peru were built on the sites of ancient temples. This is a facade of the Church of Santo Domingo, built on the remains of Coricancha, or the Temple of the Sun. It is said that the walls of this temple were completely covered with gold. The cult of the sun was the official religion throughout the empire. It was closely linked to the sovereigns, who were believed to be the sun's descendants. For this reason, they were known as the "Sons of the Sun."

A Unique Postal Service

Inca messengers or mail carriers, known as *chasquis*, were chosen from among the swiftest and best-trained youths of the nation. They had to run on foot in the shortest time possible over the highways of the empire. From four to six *chasquis* lived in cabins set along a road. Two were always posted at the threshold, one looking one way, one looking the other. As soon as one noticed a messenger approaching, he set out to meet him. Then he would turn back again, and as they ran side by side, he received an oral message, or perhaps a *quipu* that the runner brought. Leaving the tired messenger at the cabin, he continued to run on alone, until he in turn could relay the message to the next fresh runner.

Thanks to this postal system, Inca messages could travel as much as 150 miles (240 kilometers) per day. To be seen more easily from a distance, the *chasquis* wore great white feathers on their heads. Before reaching the cabin where the relief runner waited, they announced their arrival on a kind of trumpet.

When there was news of some serious event that required the help of the army, the first messenger lit a bonfire beside his cabin. When the flames and smoke were seen at the next cabin, those *chasquis*, too, lit a bonfire. Thus, one after another, the fires flashed the news all the way to the capital. When the news reached the emperor, he could dispatch his armies to the province from which the word had been sent, even before he learned the actual cause of the alarm.

The crops raised on the lands of the Sun had two destinations. Some was used for religious rituals and some went to feed the priestly class.

Produce from the lands of the Inca went to the imperial family. In addition, much of this food was stored to feed the people in times of hardship. People who could not work because of physical disabilities, illness, or old age were always fed and cared for.

The lands of the Community supported the peasants. This land was divided among families according to their needs. From time to time, the people's needs were reevaluated and adjustments were made. Since the quality of the land varied from place to place, every effort was made to insure that each family would be able to raise enough food to meet its needs.

The Government and the Quipu

The Inca government made endless use of the common people's labor. They were the ones who cultivated both the lands of the Inca and the lands of the Sun. Able-bodied men served in the Inca army, and many also labored on public projects such as irrigation canals, roads, and public buildings.

To keep a tight control over the people and their work, the government conducted regular inspections and census counts. The *quipucamayoc* were the officials in charge of information about the people of the empire. They kept careful records of births, marriages, and deaths. They also kept track of those who were ill or unable to work.

A Nation of Architects
The buildings that stand today in Machu Picchu (*above*) show us that the Incas had enormous skill as architects. The lower right photo shows a portion of the ramparts surrounding the fortress. At left is a drawing of a *quipu*. The knots represent specific amounts and their multiples.

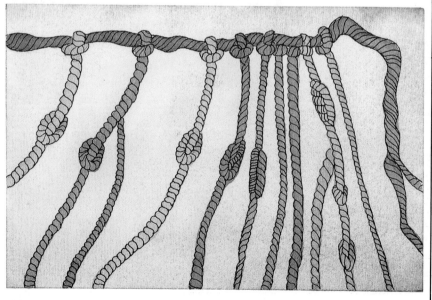

20

The use of writing was unknown in the Andean culture. But the Incas invented a unique system of record keeping, the *quipu*. The *quipu* allowed officials to make records of a wide range of information.

The *quipus* consisted of colored cords on which knots were tied according to a special system. The knots represented certain amounts and their multiples. Each color had meaning, too, according to the type of record being kept. Colors could stand for land, people, animals, and so on. On occasion, *quipus* were used to note important historical events.

Religion

The Inca community was deeply religious, and daily life was ruled by supernatural forces. These forces were worshiped by religious cults.

The supreme god, or creator and organizer of the world, was Viracocha, whose name means "Sea Foam." Viracocha rose from Lake Titicaca, one of the Incas' important sacred places.

After he created the earth and the heavens, Viracocha made human beings. Later, he created domestic animals and croplands, so that the people could survive. According to tradition, Viracocha then went to the coast and disappeared into the sea, following the path of the sun. But he promised the people that he would return.

The sky-gods were next in importance. Inti, the god of the sun, was supreme among them. The cult of Inti was made official throughout the empire. Inti was guardian of the crops and also founder of the dynasty of Inca emperors, the descendants of the sun. For this reason, emperors were called the Sons of the Sun.

There were also deities of thunder, the moon, the earth, and the sea. The moon goddess was the wife of the sun god. She ruled over cycles of fertility, both for humans and for agriculture.

Besides these official gods, there were regional, local, and family deities. Among the most important cults was the cult of the *huacas*. A *huaca* was any object, person, or natural phenomenon with such unusual traits that it was considered supernatural. A stone, a spring, or a strange animal could take on divine character. The city of Cuzco, things associated with the emperor, the snow-capped Andes—all these were *huacas*. Especially important among the *huacas* were the *mallqui*. The *mallqui* were the mummified remains of the founder of an *ayllu*. When the founder was a mythical figure, the *mallqui* was a stone statue. By preserving these *mallqui*, each *ayllu* affirmed its own identity, insuring the unity of the group.

Stargazers
Crowning the fortress at Machu Picchu is an astrological observatory. It consists of four terraces, topped by the solar clock seen in the top photo. This clock was known as the *Intihuatana*. To reach it, one had to climb seventy steps carved from a single block of granite. The lower photo shows the remains of a stairway.

22

Other religious objects were the *conopas*, small family idols worshiped to insure the fertility of people, animals, and croplands. These idols represented the desired babies, corn, peppers, llamas, and so on.

Fertility ceremonies were very elaborate, with valuable offerings of gold, silver, and fine weavings. Llamas were sacrificed, and corn was burned or spilled in the form of *chicha*, a fermented drink. These rituals marked the agricultural cycle from equinox to solstice. One of the most important sacred days was the *Inti Raymi* or Festival of the Sun, celebrated with the June solstice.

Religious rituals often included sacrifices. Animals were most commonly sacrificed, but human sacrifice was sometimes practiced, too. The purpose of these rituals was to insure good crops, the health of the people, and the well-being of the Inca Empire.

The Historical Sanctuary of Machu Picchu

Long before its discovery by the archaeologist Hiram Bingham, "the lost city of the Incas" was overgrown with vines and brambles. Then in 1911, after a long search, Bingham at last caught his first glimpse of the marvelous temples and stairways of the great fortress of Machu Picchu.

The city stands at 8,530 feet (2,600 meters) above sea level, on the eastern slope of the Andean mountain range, about 30 miles (50 kilometers) northwest of Cuzco.

In a wild region of steep mountains, high above the canyons of the Rio Urubamba, unknown workmen built a majestic city of stone. The city has given rise to countless questions that have never yet been answered. Who built it? When, and for what reason? Who lived there?

Hiram Bingham believed that Machu Picchu was built early in the Inca Empire. Other archaeologists, however, believe that the settlement existed long before the Incas arrived. According to this theory, the city was inhabited by a tribe that came from the Amazon region, probably the Chancas tribe. Still other researchers believe Machu Picchu was built in the last days of the Inca Empire. They suggest that the Inca sovereigns may have fled there to escape the invading Spaniards.

All of these ideas are only guesses. When it comes to Machu Picchu, everything is a mystery. Even its name was buried with its people. The name Machu Picchu was given in recent times, referring to the mountains that protect the city.

Mountain Paradise
Some of the peaks surrounding Machu Picchu rise more than 3,100 feet (5,000 meters) above sea level, though the average is from 7,545 to 11,800 feet (2,300 to 3,600 meters) in height. Temperatures in this region are moderately high. The humidity is high as well, but seldom approaches the extremes of the Amazon jungle.

At the entrance to the city stands a ruined watchtower that looks out over the Urubamba Valley. The sacred plaza is still visible, with three religious buildings. These are the great temple; the main temple, with three windows facing the east; and the living quarters of the priests. At the city's highest point stands a solar observatory.

The entire city looks like a fortress. Located high in the crags of the Andes, it holds a position of natural defense. Adding to these defenses, the city's builders surrounded Machu Picchu with a moat. They also built two ramparts—wall-like fortifications—that are 16 feet (5 meters) high and 3 feet (1 meter) thick.

Like other structures in the city, the ramparts are built of great blocks of stone fitted together without the use of mortar. In its great simplicity, this style is typical of Inca architecture. The builders were so expert that their work has survived both the passage of time and the jarring of earthquakes, so frequent in this region.

The main streets were arranged in steps, like a great central staircase from the lower lever to the summit. The mountainsides were carved into terraces for croplands.

When archaeological excavations began in the early 1900s, about 170 skeletons were found. Some 150 of these were of women.

Perhaps these were the "Virgins of the Sun," the women who cared for the temple. Perhaps the "lost city" was an important sanctuary.

For now, there is no test to prove these theories. Machu Picchu, fortress and sacred city, remains a mystery.

The City of Cuzco

Over time, the city founded by the mythical Manco Cápac became the administrative, political, religious, and artistic center of the Inca Empire. Earlier, various ethnic groups settled in the region, but none of them rose to prominence. With the arrival of the Incas, the city reached untold splendor. Traces of its grandeur can still be seen today.

The Spaniards were greatly in awe of the Inca capital, which they captured in 1533. Spanish chronicles describe Cuzco as "the richest city in the Indies, because it was filled with treasure for the grandeur of the gods."

The Heart of the City
The Plaza de Armas in Cuzco is the heart of the city, a clear testimony to the era of the Spanish viceroys. Most of its buildings were constructed between 1532 and 1821, and are typical examples of Peru's colonial architecture. All of the buildings in Cuzco are low, due to the frequent earthquakes. The photos show various views of the Plaza de Armas. Cuzco's Baroque Cathedral is also found here.

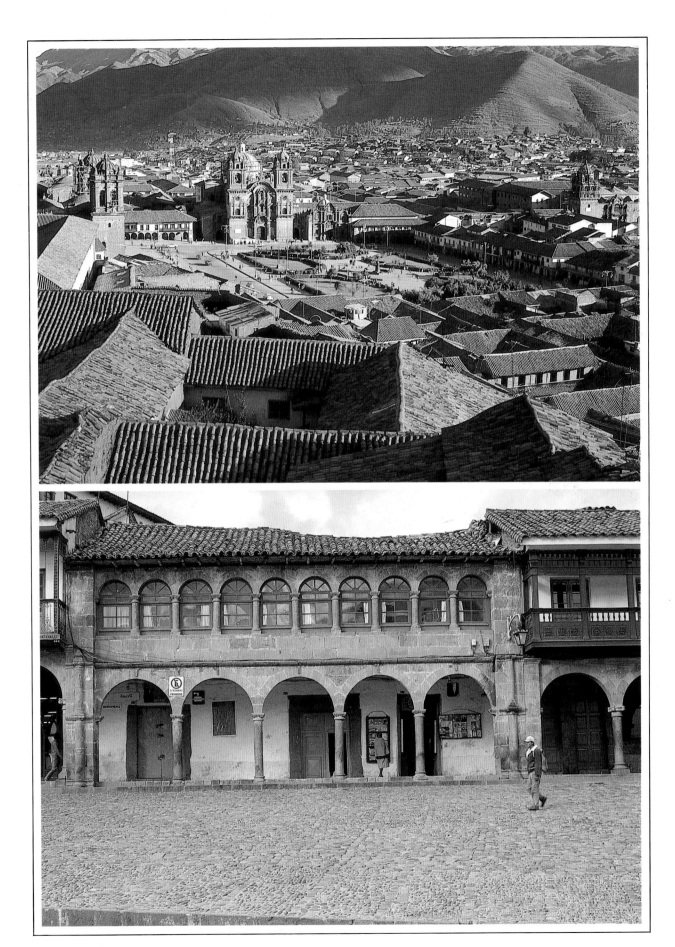

The Inca Heritage

Present-day Cuzco still has the structure of the Inca capital. Most of the buildings were modeled by the Spaniards who, under Francisco Pizarro, conquered the city in 1533. Cuzco still has many traces of the era when it shone as the capital of the Inca Empire. The descendants of the "Sons of the Sun" bear the legacy of their ancestors. The photo shows a view of Cuzco's scenic city marketplace.

"The sons of nobles from every province flocked to this court, famous for its service and adornments," the Spanish chroniclers wrote. "There were expert silversmiths and goldsmiths who worked the precious metals sent to them by the Incas. The houses were well built and often had towers, for the city was the greatest and best provided in all the kingdom. And as the Incas were rich and powerful, some of their buildings were covered with sheets of gold."

According to the sixteenth-century chronicles, Cuzco was built by some fifty thousand laborers over a period of twenty years. The buildings that the Spaniards admired so highly were the work of great architects and stone masons.

Working with enormous blocks of stone, the Inca builders showed an amazing level of skill. The outer surface of each stone was chipped so that it was slightly convex, or outward-curving. This created a smooth, billowy appearance.

As in other structures in the empire, the great walls were built without mortar. Nothing was added to fill the gaps between stones. Instead, the surfaces of the stones were cut with many angles so that they fit together perfectly, like the pieces of a jigsaw puzzle.

The city centered around the *huacaypata*, the great plaza from which spread the four royal roads. Each road led out to one of the four regions of the Inca Empire. These regions were the Chinchasuyu to the north, the Collasuyu to the south, the Antisuyu to the east, and the Contisuyu to the west. Around the plaza stood the imperial palaces.

The most important building in Cuzco was the Coricancha, the Temple of the Sun. Inside was a great disk in the shape of the sun, made of gold and precious stones.

Beside this temple stood the Temple of the Moon. There were also temples dedicated to the stars, the rainbow (Cuichi), and the lightning (Illapa).

The streets of the central city were narrow and regular, cut at right angles. The entire city was surrounded by an embankment between two rampart walls.

Many ancient Inca buildings were used as foundations for Spanish colonial structures. The Spaniards simply built on top of the ancient Inca ruins. A number of original Inca walls can still be seen, too. Some of the walls of the fortress of Sacsahuaman, on the outskirts of Cuzco, are old Inca structures that are still preserved.

Reminders of Inca Civilization
The upper left and lower photos on the opposite page show two buildings in the city of Cuzco. At the upper right are archaeological remains of the fortress of Machu Picchu. UNESCO has declared both places to be World Heritage Sites because of their fundamental importance to the Inca civilization. Cuzco also possesses important examples of Spanish colonial architecture.

These Sites Are Part of the World Heritage

Historic Sanctuary of Machu Picchu (Peru): Fortress and sacred city of the Incas. It is located some 30 miles (50 kilometers) northwest of Cuzco, on the eastern slope of the Andes, in the region called "the Brow of the Jungle." It was discovered in 1911 by the archaeologist Hiram Bingham. Its granite buildings are arranged on steps up the mountainside.

City of Cuzco (Peru): Capital of the Inca Empire. For the Incas, it was both an administrative and a religious center. From it extend four imperial roads, leading toward the four points of the compass. This city was home to the Inca kings. It had splendid civil and religious buildings. The annual Festival of the Sun was celebrated in its main plaza.

Glossary

adapt: to make changes because of a new situation

alliance: an official friendship or partnership

archaeologist: a scientist who learns about past cultures by digging up and studying their remains

census: an official count of the number of people in an area

cordillera: a mountain range

deity: a god

domain: the area over which a king rules

dynasty: a family that remains in power for a long time

elite: a superior class of people

equinox: the day in spring and fall on which there are exactly twelve hours between sunrise and sunset

excavation: a place where earth has been dug up to uncover buried things

fertility: the ability to reproduce

hereditary: passing down from parent to child

imperial: having to do with an emperor

insignia: a special mark, badge, or sign

legitimate: true or proper

meditation: centering one's thoughts on one subject as a religious exercise

moat: a deep, water-filled ditch built around a castle or city for protection

monogamous: having one wife

mortar: a soft building material that hardens over time, used to fill the gaps between bricks or stones

mummified: dried and preserved for burial

nutritional: offering great food benefits

shrouded: covered

siege: a military campaign or blockade against a fortified spot that lasts a long time

solstice: the longest day of summer and the shortest day of winter

sovereign: a king or other chief ruler

staple food: a food used constantly or in large quantities

tassel: a dangling bunch of cords or threads

tiara: a crown or headband decorated with jewels or flowers

tuber: a fleshy root or underground stem

Index

Page numbers in boldface type indicate illustrations.

Titles in the World Heritage Series

The Land of the Pharaohs
The Chinese Empire
Ancient Greece
Prehistoric Rock Art
The Roman Empire
Mayan Civilization
Tropical Rain Forests of Central America
Inca Civilization
Prehistoric Stone Monuments
Romanesque Art and Architecture
Great Animal Refuges
Coral Reefs

Photo Credits

Front Cover: Jaume & Jordi Blassi/Incafo; pp. 3-7: Jorge de Vergara/Incafo;
pp. 8-13: J. & J. Blassi/Incafo; pp. 14-15: J. de Vergara/Incafo; p. 17: J. & J. Blassi/
Incafo; p. 19: J. de Vergara/Incafo; pp. 20-23: J. & J. Blassi/Incafo; pp. 24-25:
J. & J. Blassi/Incafo, J. de Vergara/Incafo; p. 27: J. de Vergara/Incafo; pp. 28-29:
J. & J. Blassi/Incafo; p. 31: J. de Vergara/Incafo; back cover: J. & J. Blassi/Incafo, J. de
Vergara/Incafo.

Project Editor, Childrens Press: Ann Heinrichs
Original Text: Cristina Gonzalez
Subject Consultant: Dr. Robert Pickering
Translator: Deborah Kent
Design: Alberto Caffaratto
Cartography: Modesto Arregui
Drawings: Olga Perez Alonso
Phototypesetting: Publishers Typesetters, Inc.

UNESCO's World Heritage

The United Nations Educational, Scientific, and Cultural Orga-
nization (UNESCO) was founded in 1946. Its purpose is to contrib-
ute to world peace by promoting cooperation among nations
through education, science, and culture. UNESCO believes that such
cooperation leads to universal respect for justice, for the rule of law,
and for the basic human rights of all people.

UNESCO's many activities include, for example, combatting illit-
eracy, developing water resources, educating people on the
environment, and promoting human rights.

In 1972, UNESCO established its World Heritage Convention.
With members from over 100 nations, this international body works
to protect cultural and natural wonders throughout the world. These
include significant monuments, archaeological sites, geological for-
mations, and natural landscapes. Such treasures, the Convention
believes, are part of a World Heritage that belongs to all people.
Thus, their preservation is important to us all.

Specialists on the World Heritage Committee have targeted over
300 sites for preservation. Through technical and financial aid, the
international community restores, protects, and preserves these
sites for future generations.

Volumes in the *World Heritage* series feature spectacular color
photographs of various World Heritage sites and explain their historical, cultural, and scientific importance.